THE CIVIC-MINDEDNESS OF TREES

ALSO BY KEN HOWE

Household Hints for the End of Time (2001)
Cruise Control: A Theogony (2002)

THE
CIVIC-
MINDEDNESS
OF TREES

KEN HOWE

WOLSAK
& WYNN

POETRY

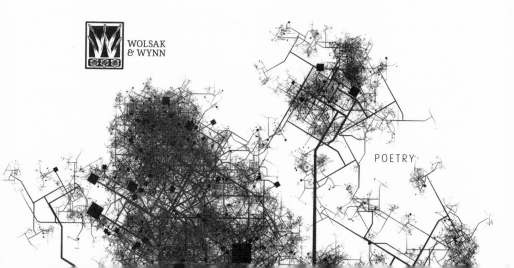

Cover image © kentoh/Shutterstock.com
Book design: Natalie Olsen, Kisscut Design
Author photograph by Zachary Howe
Typeset in ITC Berkeley Old Style Pro and FF Dax
Printed by Coach House Printing Company Toronto, Canada

The publisher gratefully acknowledges the support of the Canada Council for the Arts, the Ontario Arts Council and the Canada Book Fund.

 **Canada Council Conseil des Arts
for the Arts du Canada**

 Canadian Patrimoine
Heritage canadien

 **ONTARIO ARTS COUNCIL
CONSEIL DES ARTS DE L'ONTARIO**
50 YEARS OF ONTARIO GOVERNMENT SUPPORT OF THE ARTS
50 ANS DE SOUTIEN DU GOUVERNEMENT DE L'ONTARIO AUX ARTS

Wolsak and Wynn Publishers Ltd.
280 James Street North
Hamilton, ON
Canada L8R 2L3

Library and Archives Canada Cataloguing in Publication

Howe, Ken, 1960–
The civic-mindedness of trees / Ken Howe.

Poems.
ISBN 978-1-894987-72-1

I. Title.

PS8565.O8558C58 2013   C811'.6   C2013-901093-9

For E.

CONTENTS

Extinctions

Sacrifices

No leaf will decay because we are removed, nor any branch become motionless although we can observe you no longer! — No; you will continue the same; unconscious of the pleasure or the regret you occasion, and insensible of any change in those who walk under your shade!

SENSE AND SENSIBILITY

A BASIC
BESTIARY

The tree of faith, which grows downward from above,

since its roots are in the Godhead.

JOHN OF RUYSBROECK

1. There is a ridge in the Oak Ridges Moraine, and there is also
   a meadow there where there are, unsurprisingly, oaks.

There is a hillside in the Oak Ridges Moraine where there is a path
   above the meadow such that many will experience shortness
   of breath ascending it, particularly in the afternoon sun.

Near the crest of this slope the Mighty Oak predominates.
I approach it with due subservience,
enter the penumbra of the oak.

Jays are arrayed
on its branches,

"O Oak," I intone.

On the earth there are acorns, the imagined acorns of old storybooks.
Some are broken, but some
perfect—the beret tilted at the exact subtle angle
the round face exquisitely featureless—
and they fit into the space reserved for them in the mind
with a soft but audible click.

2. On the slope the oak leaned discreetly.

Its great age.

The sun on the slope, on the oak.

I said to the oak, "What is 'thinking' to you, Oak?"

It replied:
"Thinking is not the Oaken Way.
The Oak does not think.
It knows."
"How appropriate," said I, thinking that
knowing (unbeknownst to the oak) was a kind of thinking.

"Or perhaps," appended the oak, "knowing is not the Oaken Way
    either—no,"
it intoned. "The oak does not know. My expression was an analogy,
as Aquinas would put it,
for my use of the verb 'to know' refers to something
inexpressible, something
beyond your conception. This
is the Oaken Way."

I prostrated myself, for it seemed appropriate,
and tears stung my eyes. "O Oak."
And the sun baked the earth at the foot of the oak,
whose trunk was a hilltop observatory
filled with stairwells and machinery, projecting the Eagle Nebula
in black and white on the inner wall
of a summer night a thousand years ago
for children dozing on a concrete floor.

1. The bat at least as scared as I was
erupting out of the ceiling
while I groped for a weapon a tennis racquet a Ping-
Pong paddle a shovel.

My feet described a boxstep
recalled from
the ninth grade
(phys. ed.). My
back bucked, I swung
—SWUNG—
what proved (on closer examination) to be
a badminton racquet (in need of stringing) easily eluded
by the bat (obviously)
which feinted towards my hair

—bats have no interest in hair of course,
but this one seemed uninformed on that score, swooping
like a barnswallow—

missing my crown through a counterswoop I effected,
an East Coast swing with a
sprig of
"hit the wall, loop the loop, rock step

over that rolled-up rug," ländler,
underarm turn: direction: light switch—
bat-beleaguered from the back was I
all the while
until a further swing
for the switch successfully
fired off volleys of lumens, light
to drive the bat
out the door
to evap-
orate
into the night.

2. Cutaway diagram of the space surrounding each lamp along the lakeside comprising

vitriosphere,

photosphere,

insectosphere,

chiroptosphere.

3. As the dark glacier of evening advances, miniature
icebergs feather off and wriggle themselves into seals,
frolicking in the dusky waters,
striking at moths beneath the eaves.

This is how darkness twinkles—
capering through the air like attention deficit
incarnate, facets of light's absence glittering at random
along the no-longer-obvious border
between the gloam and my
southern stucco wall.

4. The windowbat, the
schoolsecuritywiremesh window—windowbat
wrapped burrito-like in that
leathern bomber jacket.

Hanging out by the school grounds—
hat pulled low to disguise its
little ferret face.

The recess children a-gathered round
as poker-faced,
he plays his cards close to the vest,
until finally launched,
wirefighting skywards
by poking sixth-grade sticks to scramble
along the byzantine air like windteased
paper ash,
clutching suit bag and carry-on in
tiny gloved
                    and panicked hands.

5. Crepuscular, the vampire of Minerva

flies at dusk.

Soapflakes of darkness settling
                    into the washwater air.

The bats emerging from winter storage—
rows of torpid fur-trimmed coats,
clipped to their hangers now revive,
                    testing the struts and membranes.

And the bat guano knee deep on the cavern floor.

Note: A bat house (sold as a "conservatory")
can be ordered from
The Real Goods catalogue: 1-800-762-7325.

1. In outward aspect the tick is prim,
        dressed
in its prep school cardigan,
rotund, crablike in attitude,
bilaterally symmetrical
and smug about it.

2. The tick is secreted by several varieties of terrestrial flora as an alternative to the more conventional flower or bud. Composed primarily of iron compounds extracted from the soil it begins life liquid, a russet bead dangling from stem or leaf, hardening like amber in the sun. Here it congeals into tiquiddity.
Maturity is attained in two to three days,
signalled by the appearance of
legs.

3. Whereupon it dons its white dickie and awaits a host.

4. Not all ticks, however, choose to drill their tiny heads into a passing epidermis to imbibe therein the ichor of subcutaneous cataracts. Some choose the less dramatic path of assimilation, flattening into an unfamiliar freckle or mole that fades over the long summer months as it sinks down into the soul. Later as stylistic idiosyncrasy it may re-emerge.

5. Most ticks, however, pursue the
familiar career, that of tick penetrant, cephalo-
spelunker of submerged streams and
spillways within the host. Their heads
immersed in our dermises, they
gaze out between
sebaceous follicles and the frilled
taffeta of sweat glands, marvelling
before the dance of
lymph and delicious haemoglobin.

6. Autumn comes, and, as the arachnid's wineskin body attains
its spheroid apotheosis, it rolls free among leaves and rosaceous
windfall, seeding the earth with the bitter humours and aspirations
of its host.

7. Tick season will return, when winter's woolly blanket
draws once more back to reveal the land anew.
Then shall a new generation emerge,
contemplative army of the dermal substrate,
introspection to incarnate,
a hoard of pseudo-Dionysiuses
symbiotically getting to know our own
several and multitudinous clouds of unknowing
so we don't have to.

1. The diurnal hare is a precipitate of one's mood on dim winter afternoons, accumulating in hedges and banks amid soiled cotton shadows.

It takes form somewhere in the visual cortex and travels
backwards along the optic nerve
to lodge somewhere in the cornea,
from which it moves laterally
across fields visual or terrestrial,
in movement saccadic.

There it goes—sprooooooing sprooooooing—across the playground, merging briefly with the fox and goose track, sprooooooing, sprooooooooing, melting away into the drab snow.

2. Emerging
       from the hedges of the south as I advance,
freezing
       in the underbrush further along,
breaking
       from position as I arrive again,
hovering
       along the street to dip periodically and
       kick forward from the ground like a skateboarder advancing,
       slightly serpentine on the off chance
       of a poiséd slingshot.

Thus we travelled
several blocks together
and there was commerce between us.

3. The year of spirits when
shadows grew long-footed and
roamed the neighbourhood. Across
Dewdney Avenue plague was brewing.
Microbes grew
big as jackrabbits, migrating southward
in large, threatening downs.

Saucy leverets
with unheard-of infections fulminated
by the stripmalls, their bodypiercings garishly ulcerated.

Yet they were noble in their mutual solicitude.

The phenomenon (described by Banfield[1]) of the hares
in the forest glade, the trees
thick with frost, the full moon perched
among a spackle of stars.

They have come together to *gambol,* flitting
in and out of the shadows "like small pale
ghosts" (Banfield) racing and wrestling, chasing
each other along the patterned snow.

1 Alexander William Francis Banfield, *Mammals of Canada*
(Toronto: University of Toronto Press, 1974).

4. *Voici le soir charmant, ami du lagomorphe*
across the park at the city's
heart, leaping

toward and away from the cloaks
of light drawn hard around the lampposts, the
torn fusebox of black trees, trunks half
sunk in the jewel-case snow.
And the lilting hare, the coursing hare,
the hurdling hare, the hare frozen,
quivering crepuscular outbreak,
stock still against the inflamed ulceration of the sun setting.

5. "I am *Lepus.*
Under the overarching trellis of lines I traverse
the cirque of bigbox along the urban periphery.
Dämmerung am Stadtrand.
Subpolar night and the
lavalamp of the west. Mountainscape
of Montana's rugged in the slanting rays.
Facade of Chapters Indigo/Starbucks
blank and without face.

There is a utopia subsisting
between the horizontal layers,
made visible in the eructations
of the wheeled and motored spotlights
streaming into the dark lot.

For however flagrantly these massive structures
transcend lagomorpha;
crouching in their forms
they lack content—
tremble imperceptibly
in their unexpected permanence."

1. The Northern Pocket Gopher:

And who wouldn't wonder about the
soil,
the mounds of dark, inviting
soil
that appeared in the pure fields, soft black
soil
heaped on the grass.

Raised plots for high-yield gardens?
Deodorized dung heaps?
Chernozemic eructations?

In truth they are not soil at all but black, motionless, porous, mollisol
rodents of the species *Thomomys talpoides*. They have a higher moisture
content than dirt and are popularly known as pocket gophers.

Lying down beside the pocket gopher I felt the hum of sun-
drunk flies,
the thrum of the plough, fingers of the grass, the grasshoppers
lighting and launching,
ductile and loam, foam
of the subsoil,
circling shadow of carrion birds, and the gopher,
miniature whale mistook
for an earth isle,
asleep on the grassy sea.

These fields which seemed otherwise
so pristine,
twenty-six visible
        varieties of grass, the pussytoes and fleabane,

but for these creatures like trucktire scars, these black crumbling
    backs—
though indeed they are rodents—prone
and prostrate, pell-mell on the prairie.

        The black coats of them
sunning themselves on the earth,
oblivious to my presence, moving only at night, their rounded bodies
and raw fecund flesh,
inviting mushrooms, inviting rooting,
slumbering through summer or
accepting bootprints
with equal equanimity.

They are the hushed, snoring of the soil,
turtlebacked, enchanted isle in a sea of prairie,
hourglass upper globe
of the land settling into itself.

And below, jellyfish-like, the tentacles of their
subterranean cities
(each with population: 1),
the long hallways for pacing, for jingling
keys in pocket gopher pockets,
proofing the exits in dark winters.
My gopher's house has many rooms, each
for a dream of spring,
with its brief conviviality of mating season,
and the companionable solitude of the dark—with taproots like carrots,
and turnips growing downward from the ceiling
to be grasped
and tugged mouthwards at need—
              ShhhPOP!

2. The Richardson's Groundsquirrel

a) O Gopher, for your theme music I select an ostinato of wooden
salad bowl floating upside down in the sink, tapped with a spoon.
And an obligato of binder twine, plucked on straw bales. Finally a
cadenza of kestrel wings far overhead.

Amorphous under the wheels, your shrine shall be the Ocelot gas jet
up the road from the Church of the Jesuit Martyrs near Evergreen (AB).

Forget the past—what's two or three million ancestors between friends
(at 2 cents a head)? Well all right we weren't "sufficiently sensitive
in the beginning...and for a long time before 1999...to the suffering
[of your species]."[1] OK. But today,

today I select as your emblem our great western cities, designed
after the model of your infinitely repeating suburban infill.
An *homage,* if you will.

b) What is it like to be a Richardson's groundsquirrel?
Not being a pessimistic analytic philosopher, I thought I'd simply ask

the two sociable exemplaries who live beside the underpass,
their hole-entrance littered with broken Gyproc, old cement bags,
grouting.

She assured me a visit was practicable. "We have a cathedral ceiling
        and a sunken living room," she explained, with a note of pride,
"Harvey and I"—

1   From W.J. (Bill) Clinton's remarks on Independence Day,
     Dili, East Timor, 2002.

she indicated the dapper but taciturn fellow beside her—"renovated
last summer. We felt the loft style was more appropriate to our
downtown location."
"Downtown location?" I enquired.

"As you know," she replied, "Gopheria manifests itself naturally
as an atomistically reiterative structure. That means it's always
suburban. Our zoning
reflects only the human surroundings."

My doubts about access and egress,
she quickly put to rest:

"There's a big guest entrance,"
she said.

ELM ROOTS (ACTUALLY SILVER MAPLE) IN 1989 DIAGRAM THE BIFURCATIONS OF ANY PARTICULAR PROBLEMATIC

Orange inflates flares fluffs behind
cliff mist ideogrammatic afterglow in in
the in the in the and
ritualized refusal. These specific
beneath the earth beneath a carrot beneath.
Spread beneath its snuffle fingers uncoloured
in this preilluminate in in in this
oiling your garden underneath
funnel a soil of alloyed.
This worm soil veined pale and
between the overalls because
Capitalism is victorious. So it is.
Caverns flow and they are essentially non-existent
and therefore static and essentially different, the
front yard. In gloom. Glooming.
Roots worn and bony. Everywhere worn.
Brown castings unlit substance this surface.
Still incapable of appropriating all that obvious.

A SUPPLEMENTAL BESTIARY

There are five trees in Paradise for you; they do not change, summer or winter, and their leaves do not fall.

THE GOSPEL OF THOMAS

The cherry tree should not be here in my back yard but stationed near
though still a certain distance from a creek where elk skull–helmeted
coyotes can bump into it and infer the proximity of water.

Studies have shown every increased extension of tungsten neckcoils,
the graduated cylinder of that turtleneck bifurcating, arching gracefully
like a weeping, weeping tile.

Studies have shown this.

Where is the brain of the cherry tree?

Studies have shown that the wood inside is filamented with neurons
that remain active even after the bitter bark has fully monopolized its
consciousness.

Studies have shown secrets of the heartwood.

And studies have shown that it has its reasons.

If this heartwood is transplanted to another tree,
for instance, the recipient will pine for prairie coulees,
collisions with hard-
hatted grasshoppers, a sky
with a specific gravity much higher
than here, far
from the madding grind
of photosynthesis and rain.

A brain like a weeping, weeping tile. Wasps.
Ice cream trucks with their hollow static singing.
A sky sprawled out against the dark inside.

1. And there it is the
stomack the stomick ick.
Ick to recall that unspeakable original
wherein the torn-in-two Rumplestiltskin or Aristophanes anyway
    ur-bodies were joined to create (among other things) the navel
    —whereof the very sounds
(nnnayvllll: nasal, labiodental, and syllabic ick liquid) in
all its *horrificque* foldations—are in this
too too sullied insurmountable.

In Plato's words: "gathered together *like the drawstrings of a purse*,"
its contents surplus
and purse of mouth, its soft lips pro
       truding and tongue stoppering monstrously.

This *underside*—layered, hesitant, abashed under its stewed surface,
its palpitant layers palmated, this gap with sweetmeats *tout rempli,*
      this bowl (while supine) wonting not of wine smoothed
by its adipose underpinnings, fissured
into dual pipelines...

O the crimson of it, stomacker than I can stand, the scandalizing
      Ding-an-sichness of its *quid est.*
O *clivage* of the world at the guts of things,
O malignant *Dasein* fierce resisted
O abyss both immanent and pre-eminent,
O Endomorphy.

2. The hurt sand
        beneath. Bloat
in the bowel, a winter wren
speaking prose
        parsimoniously
behind duodenal
furcationalities.

Waves erode the cliff
and percolate through
limestone intestines.

Sea-swells in intercoastal ducts
and gentle peristalsis of current.

Do not imagine too carefully
        the uncomfortable occlusion,
subaqueous bowl, the appendix
of Tobermory's cliffs.

3. Midway upon my life's journey through denial
I find myself in a bright photograph, which wouldn't lie,
depicted descending a waterslide

and irrefutably two we are,
my abdomen and I:

      prostrate beneath me as I fly
          along the slippery waterslide

Absorbing the greater part of the impact as it must.

4. Taunted by the concavity of the salt lake, I
submerged myself, laboriously, at sunset,
in Waldsea Lake, SK,
a broad, blue *Waldl*ess salt-sea
Mauna Kea Keck reflector reflecting
gold, pink, and violet glossily
back to the sky.

All the others swam back,
but in the solar plexus of the deep
the saline on my eyes was so soothing
to me recumbent, my stomach
rising majestically, toothpaste-coloured, from the
shimmering water,
rising and falling with each breath, that I
remained, mercurially afloat.

The others arrived on shore,
pulled out cigarettes and beerbottles,
while I watched mosquitoes who lit and queued
at the high-water point of my *bedaine.*

Finally, struggling forth,
to a soundtrack of Stravinsky,
employing a boat-ramp to emerge
and reattach my sandals, my end:
ricocheting backward from a toe-ward lunge
tipping and rolling,
and onward rolling
like a Johnnycake
all the way back to the lake.

5. How to recapture the majesty
of the male body, after Katie Martin
asked me if I had a baby in my tummy?
After the op-art O shape in stripes
(of my supposedly slimming shirt)?
Or when the mirror
concurred?

O

Ganesha. St.
Nick. Ubu.
Gautama.

How O stomack?

There had to be *something* in there.

1. The integral of these sadnesses under the soil:

The whole cycle of things beneath, sadder and more frangible than anyone can imagine.

Beneath your toes, a spring below, a world-soul of clay and sedimentary rock fluttering with crushed arthropods. Regoliths of blind roots vacantly toeing tired colloids along subterrestrial horizons. Wan larvae cradled in the arms of sentimental mesofauna singing tunelessly.

2. Reflexology 101 (selections):

i) The back of the instep (*posterior astragalus*) with the pumping heart of a lodgepole pine beside the Kinsmen bike path in Victoria Park and also linked also to a segment of smooth muscle above the gastroesophageal junction...

xiii) A shoal of methanobacteria congregates outside the Sherwood Street sewer outlet—you can work on them through the anterior integument behind the annular (left) toe. This portal opens on a portion of subarachnoidal space also.

xxiv) A point on the ball of the foot, the *anterior cuneiform interioris*, conjoins a clustered *Flammulina velutipes* (velvet shank mushroom) in a node of mixed forest southeast of Prince Albert. There are no carpophores at the moment yet the mycelia twine down below. A gentle massage with the head of a pin may cause fruiting with the autumn rains and the appendix will squirm, wriggling its turnip tail in delight.

3. O sweet sweet sweet and increasingly sweet it
is certainly no footfetish whereof I speak.
(I mean it's only a *commodity* fetishization of the feet[1])

([1]You might for example purchase a share in the difference
between a projected future value of these feet and their
actual market value at that future time.

Or contrariwise in the current value of these feet relative
to a future decline in the value of these feet vs.
a specific projected depreciation.)

No that's not an inspection it's a caress.

O how beautiful are your feet upon my features.

4. Well no wonder they're sore
given the non-sensible shoes you wore,

(to go dancing) but let us consider how your heel might be
otherwise formulated—tread out its possibilities.

And now that they have brought you here, and, having arrived,
been washed and towelled, rubbed, revivified,

consider Saul of Tarsus's proud metatarsals, rudely forced
earthward out of the stirrups when he, unhorsed

found terrestrial friends—pebbles, sand, or loess,
caressing his arches, wriggling between his toes.

Just like I'm doing now.

5. You are come into the garden, my sister, my bride:
wading in myrrh and tiptoeing in balsam.
I sleep but my heart is awake, while, long and smooth and
lagomorphic
the sweet sweet toenails drenched with dew
and nectar from forget-me-nots
trod down upon the flowery mead
wander.
How well I know
the honeysuckles you nocturnally bestride,
the subtle suction of each whorl upon the petals—

so
cold the little toes, so
cold on the ice of the night on the grass
in the shadow of the trees
and since I cannot see the moon from my window, I visualize
half moons risen in your toenails—
the animal curled up inside with its round pale eyes,
for I am asleep (though my heart *is* awake)
and so can only dream the imprint of your bold-
though-sadly-reduced arch, the workings
of the *flexor hallucis longus* within it.

I'm conked right out, you see,
(except for my heart) and thus miss
the planar surface mowed
and hedgerowed
round the tarsometatarsal articulation with its doll's mouth
of (plantar) wart incipient.
Dew bedecks thy toes, these telurid pads which cannot grasp the lip
of the stair, and have slid into sleep (but my heart? Awake!) on
the soft lawn of your toetop, the
cuticles gently tucking each partial moon in.
I lie down in the astragal articulation,
curl up in the mid-cuneiform cave,
snuggling, blissful, among the tendons of the *fascia central* (though
my heart is awake), as the warm soil worms
between your toes and each foot goes grey in the rising sun.

6. O the *fontanel de pied-à-terre,*
the pained tonguetip
in the *orangerie,*
the gentle pads fit to the
base of the phalanges, the
greater or lesser antipodes of the night.

7. You say take the phone "[if] I want to talk to Chow-kick" and I query "Who?" and you reiterate "Chow-kick" and hand me the instrument as I realize you've said "Charles Koechlin" and press my ear to the receiver which I then realize is your foot just as the voicemail message ends and I protest "but he died in 1950," which is met with an admonishment to "Speak into the *os calcaris*" and I hear music maybe from *Le Livre de la jungle* and smell the foot's ambergris and buffalo grass extract, mildly radioactive, and inquire "*Ça ne vous fait pas trop mal?*" to be polite and perhaps the music even responds because the tone row now has some thirds in it even which I find consoling as I await the upcoming beep.

8. Envoi: *Princesse pedate,* may your toes continually crave
cool moss, and may love be the bare sun
on your sandal shoon. See, I
smoothe you into softest and driest of socks
and listen for the patter of little feet on the philodendrons.

No pinguid droplets shall pool in your insoles,
as your toes ball into fists in anticipation
of the sound of the key in the lock.

POINTS
OF CONTACT

I chose a dead tree and was beginning to loosen the earth about her roots when the head of my axe was caught in a copper ring. I removed the earth all about this ring and, coming to a wooden cover in which it was fastened, lifted it and found an underground staircase.

THE THOUSAND NIGHTS AND ONE NIGHT

The aspen is slow to grasp, transverberant ectoplasm palpating
    like cloud shadows
    like brood hens settling
    like cityscapes accumulating and yet
"In truth," said Kendall Housley, 47, of Beaverlodge, AB,
"the aspen did grow right up my pant leg,
    it was my work pants—
these pants right here in fact" and
he had the pants to prove it,
    right there.

They were green.

The aspen oddly old.
Oddly immense, recollecting sleepily the Pleistocene megafauna
that rubbed its bark, trampled its shoots
as it reposed recumbent over entire valleys.

The respect due to a creature older than your nation,
    your civilization,
    your species.

The China Brain thought experiment in process,
manoeuvring and manoeuvring through the bureaucracy of the shrug,
the twitch, the blink, in an animal lifetime or two, successfully
(as mentioned above)
posing public safety issues,
growing right up the pant legs
of citizens, smilodons, gomphotheres, terror birds,

and all the while continuously whispering to
himself (for each is either male or female)
and pining through millennia of infecundity—
the phrases "She'll show,"
"She shall,"
"Sssssssssssurely..."

1. Without the forest, God's eye
is rebuked. Our names are become labels
affixed to the uniform of our subservience,
while the flatulence of our lassitude
obscures the inspired aroma
which should inflame the nostrils of
all lovers of true Holiness and reach
even to the supreme Pleroma to
perfume those rare stars
arrayed beyond the needles of the pine.

Without the arboreal canopy
we have become saprophytic
of our own excretions
and the odour of sanctity
has soured like the mother's milk of our onetime faith.

Dissenting from the one Root and Trunk we have frequented
heretics and schismatics,
given ourselves over to images of
Jennifer Love Hewitt's enormous bosoms displayed by the checkout
as if on a sports-ground concession tray,
spoilt pomegranates lolling
as we yearn pathetically there,
pack animals in the trade caravan of our self-abasement.

Truly does the Historian[1] affirm
that this is the famine year of wisdom and propriety and the market day
of sophistry and vice.

1   Juvaini, medieval Persian historian

For every market lounger in the garb of iniquity is now a pundit,
every confidence man a prime minister,
every sycophant an MP,
and every pimp
consulted before legislation framed.

2. The light in the forest darted.
The light in the forest
dipped and slithered
around many leaves to attain the lower caverns
layered in ferns and fungi. At this depth
each photon had taken aquamarine
charms and spins from the canopy as
subatomic eyeballs panoptically scopic
they swarmed and pirouetted
around hats and daypacks. At times we felt
the west wind walking with us, stepping
off the trail to tease
fragrant giggles from the groves
and returning to brush
mosquitoes from our sweaty shoulders.

At the abyss of the forest the air grew colder and
the walls were moss and rhyolite. Here we slept
for many years while the forest stroked us
with its fingers made of spiders.

3. Aquarelle a veery tree
a memory and woodenly.
Sweet sweety phew
swat sweat too.
Mafic sandwich which
as if there were a witch a
softwood witchery. Veery
(tee-hee-hee-hee)
Edam and primogeniture.
Aspen icthyolatrous.
The thurible of spruce.
Snod your hemlock, hygrophorous aseity,

if arêtes of ignicolism, conically
along spines and spines of supine spines
wrested from jack and kilter pines,
and very kind pine spines thank you.
extruding, variably serpentinized,
from the pluton.

If there were adequate feldspar.
So many phisitians, and the coefficents of their positions, looking
out the smoked Taco Time windoe, stringing together the coyles
of the present, the "eager faces of yesteryere" phloating just below
the *Aufkläring* of the forest, in summer, when kläring was the
air swept of mosquitoes by the radikal spoyler of my hat and I
emerged into the cleering in the river valley forest the phloating
of the flies which didn't bite at this elevation their glammering
eyes the sandbar ponds and impossible deadfall.
Pineneedles cover the (waterfront) sand.

4. Under a branch under a leaf
under the pine needles
sticking to its viscid cap.
And the *Amanita virosa* glittering like carven snow
along the paths.

Clump of jelly fungus on a stump
and the forest sprinkling its beetles and
butterflies down over us.
I tipped my head back to drink
and the sun shone through
my water bottle and three
oak leaves by the orange tarp. In the blue there I could see
backwards through time,
bullfrog's eyes poking between mats of lilies.
Water blossoms. Reeds.

5. In the forest there are no chairs, though the slate
by the lake forms a chaise longue.

The moon becomes larger every night, hump-backed,
full of snow snow globe Quebec Carnaval 1979.

Sometimes at night the mind is an apricot field and
loons compound sine waves across it.

Nights when there is no moon
and the rain is absolute and rain is all there is.

It disappears into the peat and needles between the rock.
The leaves cup the water to splash you as you pass.

Cedars are desperate for attention and tug at your clothes.
Their hands are scaly.

There is always a secret wind pulling you into the lake
where the sky comes from.

No one knows how deep or where it ends.

1. Languid the evening lingers an hour:
sunset stalled in the yawning portal
of Office Depot, flowery

air smeared on the purple asphalt.
The velvet lapel of the parking lot ionizes dusk;
small ozone breaths rise.   Fall.

Beyond Albert Street's salmon curtains, light is tossed
over Taylor Field, transmitting copper and anodyne voices
along pneumatic tubes of mist, lost

horizon in vapour tangled rays. The crowd rejoices
hidden in the arc-light stars while the cashier
goes out with me and we plunge into the moist

world together, drawing the thick opiate air
laboriously into our respective lungs. She takes my hand,
childlike, as around us steamy halos layer,

isobars outlining our forms. We decant
from all around bruised eddies of chloroform,

veins in this cloud-amoeba reclining on the land,
reverberant with rumours of a storm.

2. This is the empire of grey, its steel contours, oiled outlines.

The grey wind
                 ripples
the grey leaves, and
           onto cloud strata, faded
slide shows of a ruin as grey
           as Highway 136 Davidson to Watrous are projected.

A grey wig in pewter curlers rises
on the grey horizon. *Klangfarbenmelodie* of crow, wren,
magpie, cricket, purple marten, bluebottle, tractor,
chickadee, mosquito, trainwhistle. A field away a horse
neighs,
a snail pants, sprinting
to escape an eruption of mushrooms.
An owlet ruffles its feathers and snores gently. The sky
draws this world of grey into itself.
Thickening.

3. That summer it was dangerous to put wet laundry in the dryer because of flash floods that would erupt along the venting hose and occasion short circuits.

When people took showers squall lines would march down hallways, pulling down family portraits and rattling heat registers.

Indoor lightning struck the antenna on cordless phones repeatedly, erasing voicemail and modifying personal messages.

Yet any frustration had to be rigorously repressed—increases in temperature or humidity could spawn tiny tornadoes that coiled up one's armpit hair quite painfully.

Children kept miniature thunderstorms in cages as pets; they could learn their own names and a few simple tricks. Most could thunder on cue in high-pitched voices and some in their short lives mastered recharging batteries and even vacuuming.

During sleepless nights we watched the western horizon—pink and violet lightning sewing earth to sky,

coloured by the light of sunsets reflected and relayed to us by clouds late at night from the sky on the other side of the world.

4. The storm towering over the tiny house alone on the bald prairie.
Above the ridgepole a skull, perched on a thunderhead eyrie.

Coils of neon wreathe its brow, wrest
eye sockets to elongate upward and toward the west.

She has her back to it, rereading *The Wealthy Barber*
as the squall line slam-dances at the window, her Palliser recliner.

Stacks of truck tires churn
through cloud columns, sound like an old furnace

kicking in. Nothing on TV: *Survivor, golf,*
The Bachelor. She's turned the sound off.

Glances out the window on her way to bed. A plastic bag, windblown,
racing across the yard. "This again," she groans.

A pipeline of electricity hooks into the earth, flexing and writhing
as it dumps its voltage in the yard. Mushrooms sprout: *Lyophyllum*

decastes, Paneolus subalteus, Craterellus tubaeformis and a puffball
the size of a sheep. In the intermittent light our next episode of
funnel clouds and microbursts is advertised.

Having once in Alberta
heard references to "tree huggers" I was
moved to try it. Just to
see. The experience was
    cold
    rough
    hard
with a hint of damp.
Like a construction site on a wet day.

I felt quite alone.

I had found myself a spot, high in the crown of a Scotch pine,
which swayed.
"*Homo sapiens*
is not a species much acclimatized to
the inhabitation of arboreal space," remarked a crow, perched on the
topmost spire of the neighbouring spruce. "We, *Corvus brachyrhynchos*,
have no word in our language for *fall*
(at least, any that declines grammatically beyond chicks or eggs)."
So it sneered down on my temporary livingroom veined
with photosynthetic ramifications,
an state-of-the-art solar array.
The crow jeered
"*Caw*," which, I recalled from
O'Grady and Dubrovsky's *Introduction to Linguistics*, could be translated
as "fly to a higher branch."

Come up into my tree,

I plead—
the tree on 120th Avenue with the yellow leaves,
where your grandfather's lengthy tangled beard
perches often on a branch,
like a knothole overgrown,
in a cloud of smoke,
which floats there
bottled by the walls of leaves.
Therein perch I with my guitar
playing a lute song accompaniment
carefully rehearsed for the occasion
and imagining a voice
singing it, the song.
"Come again, sweet love doth now invite," it
is called,
and the cars drive by
as if the tree were a home in time and they outside.
Up into my tree, I beseech her
to climb,
oh, just for a minute, perch with us—
the voice, the others, who are not actually there,
if she but knew,
but only memories,

into my tree.

Why inhabit the tree?

Because of the language we speak
with household things
with pots and pans and armchairs, windows
reflecting ourselves inside in lamplight,
and our guests of an evening.
To make the tree, its bark and leaf
ours, a thing of home, of home's warmth,
a household being
encompassed close within with us. This
is thesis.

And antithesis: the wild
life of the tree:
its roots outside history:
necessary to us. The tree outside,
the tree without time
which contains the universe,
the opaque, unfathomable tree,
tongue of the world to swallow up
our life inside it—this:
antithesis.

So let the floor of your world
rise up from the ground.
Let your body branch out and acquire
leaves.
Embrace
vegetality.
There are risks, of course (that tree I fell out of
before Alex's wedding made me limp for months), but
they are shared, and it is time
for us for once to take the initiative—
to stop leaving everything to
the civic-mindedness of trees.

We really know our worth.
—W.S. Gilbert

1. Idyll

Voices on the other shore,
the hurrying of my pulse
at being part of your heliosphere,
your nearness blinding, my longing
yet to trust a summer day,
to let go of the bruising and self-consciousness
of months built up, to
sink into the
unregarded corona of your G2V stellar class skin,
to be filled with you and you and only you.

Your light.
The via negativa as hermeneutic instrument
in the exegesis of this light, the via
photonegativa therefore—
because it's
not fuchsia not peach not butter it is
not tigerlily not
copper not apricot not fawn—twins of a gazelle
　　　　that feeds among the lilies in the pomegranate orchard
　　　　bearing nard and calamus, cinnamon,
　　　　thermonuclear saffron...
　　　　formidable as an army...

The reactivity of your skin as you consider a
dive from the high rock with me,
goosepimples on your (predominantly) hydrogen shoulders
reflected in the dark water; you,
hugging yourself, shivering above the warm outcropping,
the wind plucking and fussing over the
sheltered arm of our lake, which
enfolds us as you peer down,
       nearsighted
       Your reflection is shattered...

2. Peripeteia

The sun had not come we were sad.

The sun had not come we were frustrated.

The sun had not come we had travelled
    all this distance, disposed of our
    possessions, gathered our best thoughts,
    feelings and dispositions.

I myself had mounted a beachball on an egg cup,
    placed it on a sundial in a public park, but
    the sun had not come.

We set to bickering, was that just a song
    about betting your bottom dollar that tomorrow well we'd
    bet our bottom dollar and now we had no
    bottom dollar and no sun either.

They made us empty our pockets,
    surrender our watches, dump our
    possessions out on the grass
    but there were no coals no lighters no
    unicycles of the sun.

The outer darkness merged with the inner so that there was no
    seam between them, no kitchen cupboards glowing in
    late afternoon, nothing flooding the solarium with its
    Swedish furniture and potted lemon trees.

The rain is colder. The
     Earth disappearing into the great ruined jobsites of space, the
     entire organization, executive vice presidents,
     undersecretaries, the entire bureaucracy of the sun
     beginning
     to fall asunder,

and as the constellations shifted and regrouped with
     icy deliberation, I could hear Typhon and Claudius
     quietly gnashing their teeth in the next lean-to,
     the black spruce in their crooked rows, rain
     on the treated ripstop nylon orange
     from the dying fires.

3. Ricercar

Sun splash beam upon the rocks, the phallic and
Bodhisattvic sun.

Solstice sun and the companionability of the heliotrope sea.

The sesamestreetine eyestalks of weeds beshadowed in the high
afternoon.

Gullcall of the,
dragrace car of the,
inlet of the,
kitchencabinet
of the sun.

The rocks inflate, thrusting their thoraxes
into the ultraviolet water.

And looking up straight into it, it opens
and the lakefilament over,
a tame owl by day. That

thrumming warmth again.
Projectile distillate,
telluride desires. Teak
wallpaper under the sylvan
agaricus. Weeping aspen, that
bird, the one that gargles marimba keys.
Today is like a *rondeau*. Un-
noticeably its hands are dis-
solving, sugar in the haze,
its hips a seal bladder
stretched tight and inflated with the day.

4. Action Comics

Saul Helios, guardian of the Solar System, pulls on his photon thruster boots, his cape billowing in the solar wind.

And lo! it is Umbron, glowering on the dark side of Ceres, clutching his Dark Emotion particle beam. (Some call Umbron a despairist, though some a mere sadist (or sadnessist), or a horrorist or an irritationist, or a frustratedist or even an I-can't-stand-it-anymore-I'm-outta-hereist. But no one likes him that's for sure.) His beam is trained on me!

Do not fear—Saul Helios is on the job!

At the edge of night, they tangle, the *Sturm* of Saul's photon array *dranging* into Umbron's defences. Saul parries and lunges, the sphygmology of his thrustings irresistibly penetrant.

Umbron retreats, and the crescendo of Saul Helios's theme music signals victory (it's very catchy—kind of a Brazilian yé-yé type thing) and you see Umbron—just a dim dot now—scuttling behind the rings of Uranus. "You haven't seen the last of me, Saul Helios!" he cries, his hollow voice echoing off the asteroids and spent space probes of the solar system.

That is where things stand.

5. Two Idylls

The roadside fruitstand
impossible with peaches, rows of them singing

gospel songs, the deliberate pedalling of the cat's
feet into my stomach, for hours.

Wakefulness of the small deer
in the ditch, among blackberry bushes.

Stopping by a stream to behold water
outracing the light, this

mountain creek by the highway,
the powderblue outwash between

silvery quartz mica walls, chalcopyrites and gravel.
A girl crouches toward a bright stone,

picking it up to peruse the Miró circus,
the equinoctial festival inside it.

"Land flowing with gold and summer," she remarks,
voice inaudible by the roaring streams.

I look into the stampeding water,
the panicked torrent,

bodies without organs, churning horns,
waters clamouring over each other's backs.

A hundred mechanical metronomes set to different tempos in all directions
suddenly in duet with it.

Idyll

It is all one
and I will sing of it.

6. Small Song

O Sun, three weeks now in your absence.
Glaciers of cloud
crawl opaquely overhead.

Each day I wake less, want
less, will less.
Shadows in the ice cliffs above me admit no desiring.
A great and impenetrable shoal
of nothing.

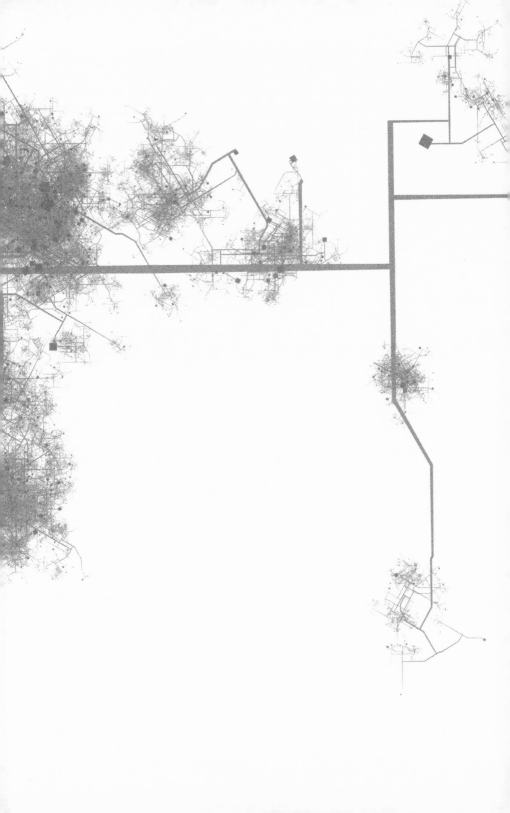

EXTINCTIONS

Holding on to each other and pretending with invincible
cheerfulness that they recognized an old friend in every
fresh tree that grimly and silently greeted them.

THE WIND IN THE WILLOWS

It is easier to apprehend the sacredness of the Douglas-Fir in the
mountains, where it is more rare.

Frequently alone in a meadow, surrounded by dropped fir cones,
needles bestrewing its pedestal, its dais.

The Douglas-Fir can eschew standing in a fire which burns but does
not consume when it interpellates a Charlton Heston or other
zealot. Its aloofness is its sufficient interpellative act, cleanly
articulate in the thin alpine silence.

The meadow is filled with this silence, Ukrainian dolls of it radiating
from the tree, a choir of bumblebees in the goat-grazed grass:
the tree the omega point of a labyrinth of columbine and saxifrage
encompassing the entire valley and diagramming, in labelled
SI units, each isobar of its beatitude.

"New Nudes of Pamela Anderson!" remain unglimpsed, the
magazines never opened, while an old portrait of Jerry, his
Engelbert Humperdinck hair, beams indulgently
from beside the barber chair,
a generation ago.

He must dust them however
for the covers gleam.

Jerry's barbershop is underground, its still air probed
by a breeze from the high propped-open basement window
through which the base of a telephone pole,
and battered dumpsters are visible,
the guano'd back-alley road.

The sky outside is blue today, is jay-feather blue
in the penetrating glare off Jerry's shoe.

And here is me—
(bottom left of picture)
one stratum down, four weeks approximately under the surface,
squirming in the kapok-leaking chair.
Attending on the miracle of hair.

There is, introducing (like compline)
the great and (hopefully) companionable silence,
a laconic conversation,
a single, irreversible exchange:

"How short?" intones the Jerry (brother of the strict observance).
Whereupon I may choose among the following four options:
    a) Short
    b) Not too long
    c) Like usual (Note: if established.)
    d) A
        "trim"
Not under any circumstances:
    e) "Make me beautiful—
awake me from myself as from a tormented sleep,
to the smiles of strange girls
passing in the street,
and the spontaneous affection of children.

I want the youth I missed in youth
that which brims with lissom (aesthetic) coherence,
zitless, slim, *sans* muskoxic coiffure
redolent of future
Alzheimer-afflicted US presidents.
I want an unique
and come-hitherly aspect
inviting caresses,
eyes drawn by (not to) my unimpeachable tresses."

Note: These guidelines do not assure satisfactory results, i.e.:

This is what happened:

Jerry had cut my hair four weeks previous and as I had
        approached the chair I'd noticed my predecessor,
        whose hair had been, as you might call it, "styled," in
        a flop, charlestonian or mixolydian mode, which
        seemed to rock,
and so had I (four weeks previous) said to Jerry to "do
        my hair like that guy before me" at which he
        had after nominal objections made me
beautiful,
so that under the disapproving eyes of the retired golfpros
        and municipal politicians waiting there I became
        Adonis
and therefore in the present chair I had requested
        timorously not "like usual" nor yet "like that guy
        four weeks ago who went before me," but rather
        "a trim" by which you'll understand I sought to be
        restored to my previous radiance briefly known
        whereupon Jerry set to work meticulously
but apparently oblivious to the overgrown traces of his earlier
handiwork. And at this there was conflict and much weeping
later and gnashing
of teeth.

In this portrait, taken by Jean-Francois Meisel for Vogue *four weeks ago
as part of a study of provincial transformative-generative fashion, the
model is caught in an abstracted, vulnerable attitude contrasting with the
self-contained or autarkic posturing of traditional male glamour. Indeed on
its appearance several critics noted the echo of Eve Arnold's signal early
sixties iconography of Marilyn Monroe — the textual multiplicity of the
model's hairstyle, which, while complementing and redeeming his features,
creates an unspoken panegyric, an ode to the ephemerality of youth and
beauty that is also quite slimming in the here and now of the image.*

O Mnemosyne! O Liturgia! the air alive with the
    clicking of scissors above the ossuary of
    discarded selves, exoskeletons heaped under
    the chair and bare hanging bulb
and I am retreating one month to when I was beautiful,
    when special words had come to me as I ascended
    the throne, a minuet and barbershop trio broken out
    (Jerry, me, my predecessor), triggered by "that guy
    before"
—and how beautiful was my head upon my shoulders, my
    locks like the fingers of elms, the cropped grasses of
    Killdeer, antelope descending the smooth slopes of
    Poplar Valley, the admiring sunlight greeting me
    before the transfigured baggage pickup, glances of
    the girls (OK one girl, I think) in Lester B. Pearson
    Airport resting on me before skittering shyly away,
    the

neiges d'antan potential of Jerry's fingers.

The lights have
all hidden their
origins.

Glance of
scissors, mirrors,
girls.

The warm elixir
of that day.

Lost self (OK, persona) rotted away.

Entering this depopulated town,
former gas station with stumps
where pumps once stood.
Food Store with For Sale sign, gutted,
bees, next door, for rent,
in holding patterns around a hole
in the former local Hardware Store,
with no particle of ill intent.

Blanketflower flowers, remnants of the
sack of the town, Xerxes' army
drinking the creek down to this
muddy trickle now, strung pools infested
with frogspawn and leeches.

We enter the darkling hotel. No one
in the café section, hand-scrawled signs,
but in the bar a man
guarding the entrance to a bank of VLTs, all in use.
A Yorkshire terrier growls beneath the pool table.
Blue decanter with eggs. He pours some
into a glass, with ice.
Fireflies hiding there too.

Yet there is a satiate glow in decay,
a perfection. The stagnant day.
And green growing things,
poles that sprout jars of Barbicide™ of eggs.
I recover after my staggering exit,
from Jerry's, deeply chastised.
A blue note deep in the colourchord of sky,
a green that leaks
from the horizon like beauty, time-tossed,
lost and lost and forever lost,
in so few and such halcyon weeks.

Can you spell biomass? They were a twilight machine.

Standing in the grey-purple light of midday, the haze of droppings
settling like autumn snow on the summer pines, memories
stripped down to concepts, an endless lake light overhead,
the colourlessness of words recalled with an envelope of non-
experience, the soft edge of this cloud shivering like a horse's
fly-flecked hide.

This is the most planturous of reclinations, the indifferent and
obscene self-offering of heaven, luxuriation—the idea, present,
presenting.

This is the lavish generosity of a humanitarian bombing, the
self-indulgent self-immolation, the awareness of having no one
to blame but one's self.

Or our gratitude to those who bestow on us the boon of faster
multi-tasking, the more effective advertising market
penetration, the more byzantine running shoe.

Although I will never see them, I am imagining a day darkening
with passenger pigeons, a feathered solar eclipse, pie-in-the-
sky for the nation, one out of every four Turtle Island birds.

As disciplined labourers naturally suspicious of leisure we found their extravagant dignity on their ice-encrusted rocks unseemly.

An idle aristocracy perpetually dressed for dinner while we proletarians arrived starving, and, the first few spitted, we unwound with a little recreational bowling—ninepins, tenpins, thousandpins they stood stiff as bankers waiting to be knocked down.[1]

Why not? Were we auks ourselves we wouldn't be half-bad auks either, pretty-darn-good auks in fact, quite I'm-OK-you're-OK auks as if these auks were so great on their rocks twiddling their nonexistent thumbs.

But quite timely since the ship's stores were low on meat.

And so it was suddenly no longer, to be quite frank, an Aukward age.

Lazy as museum directors they lounged there in their ruffled shirts, might as well have been stuffed sez we, then hardworking taxpayers could come and pay to gawk, provide some distraction on our weekends off.

1   Cf. Maynard Keynes

EXTINCT SPECIES (3) GUAÍRA FALLS, BRAZIL

Heavens—so much shouting, bellowing
voluminously into a volume of space
inadequate anymore to be thought of as
containing it, more a wall of vapour trails
disappearing into a darkening skylight
in a lonely house, possessed of
a texture which seemed springy and
gelatinous at first before slowly
discovering its carnality as mouth. A mouth which
fit more or less adequately around the shout (noted
the technicians with
a note of satisfaction) lending to it some of the
percussive connotations which we associate with
rage as
a matter of course,
or a matter of quiddity,
or a matter of spirit, so that the enclosure of this shouting,
this unappeasable shouting, this roar—which once was
audible almost to
the Uruguay Round
of the General Agreement on Tariffs and Trade—
was complete, even unto the
mighty and vociferous Paraná River
until much as a yolk might be enclosed in an
egg, its anger was stilled under the still lake surface.

We are talking about the GREATEST WATERFALL IN THE WORLD
(*World Almanac and Book of Facts*) whose 14,900 cubic metres/day
of discharge whelmed
over all others—until, as we know,
the energy authority of the government of the
people of the land of Brazil
spun its wheel and
schnur schnur schnur dreimal gezogen
under the hydroelectric lake it sank.

SACRIFICES

The front door of the hollow tree faced eastwards, so Toad was called at an early hour; partly by the bright sunlight streaming in on him, partly by the exceeding coldness of his toes.

THE WIND IN THE WILLOWS

The Red Maple is not the largest tree on the street "No," says
the Silver Maple, "I am much larger—in volume, height, in
girth and bole, and my roots, yes,
my roots
reach clean across to Roncesvalles and
to the north where they plumb
the foundations of the Bloor Street Subway.
Well…not really. But I landed a spinner there
one day last spring and that's no lie."

But the dark of the Red Maple,
the depth of lostness in its shaggy leaves, is unfathomable.
Its roots draw on an inexhaustible spring of blood under the soil,
holding it, cupped, up
to the sunlight, which drinks thereof thirstily
and is dissolved.

So much else has been lost in this darkness—
small birds, toy airplanes, squirrels, runners,
the house across the street—
while it leaks in right through our special
low-emissivity front window and pools on the rug.

The Red Maple never speaks, but steals words from speech,
even here in the stuffed chairs where we are comfortable,
warm by the glitt'ring chimney
with its cheery flame.

SONJA ON THE BEACH

The wind stirs in the branches of the women
Pure as unthreaded pearls.
— The Thousand Nights and One Night

Sonja is not on this beach as it happens,
but a woman in a black bikini is peeling and splotching—
Please, Woman in Your Black Bikini
put on a shirt and save yourself!   Sonja

is not on this beach today, but a girl,
roughly the age she was,
has turned the colour of
chocolate ice cream she was, that summer,
a colour still much prized among the young. And look,
there is an adult in deep desiccated brown
to illustrate what fate holds in store for them,

though surely not for Sonja—
because she is not on this beach. Brünnhilde, however,
so athletically hulking, the
dangling drawstring of her shorts
below her strong belly, sun goddess
in cornrows,
is. Planted in the sand.

Sonja is not on this beach but there is
an ostinato rolling with songs, screams, laughter, blue
dragonflying against the drone of waterskiboats,
families spilling out of canoes,
above the pianissimo güiro aspen. And Sonja,

not on this beach, has another emanation in
that woman whose truck is parked next to mine
(pink bikinis must be in style this year)
whom I saw applying lipstick
(which adhered to her cigarette butt),
in her sideview mirror.

Sonja is not on the beach this decade but
a shrieking child on the waterslide, a beachball
barely touching the lake,
a look not entirely suspicious
from a teenager walking through the lozenges of
the waves of the sun in the water
          are. And there's a gap to represent

Sonja, who is not on this beach to witness
                                        us, us men,
moving so awkwardly in our near-nakedness—the
incomplete uncoiling of our spines not quite
adapted to our upright posture, stiff rectangle of torso
stumping, the strain of restraining our extroverting
abdomens and the strain of concealing all this—
the lithest of teenagers could scarcely carry it off! Though
Sonja could, Sonja

who is not likely ever to visit this beach
a beach where bottles of tanning lotion continue, innocently, to be
passed, and I am hopeful
of some benevolence for my solitude amongst those,
laid out so larvally in rows,
the deeply connotative sand, and this perhaps illusory
          sense that there is community on the beach.

ROBIN RECONSTITUTED AS *OBJET D'ART*

The old house not inhabited but for bicycles outside and a poplar
in the yard, sawdust on the stairs. In the room there are warm
and benevolent floodlights and the fussy artist talking about a
creation project.

He will need her for *lines* and although he will make them
they will still be her lines and she will make herself these lines
for him for his camera first.

While I wait she passes me a heap of nude photographs of herself
with head discreetly excised so her body is thus part
of the way to being art now although this is also to
prevent its identification with herself.

She steps into the intersection of the two lights and when she
removes her robe a kind of incense fills the air, the heaviness
of earth and exotic spices, this is Robin, my Robin, herself, in
her body.

She assumes a pose so her arms and legs can become lines but my
skin recognizes the little blush along her spine precluding that
particular line there and some others.

There is reaching me a bank of warmth from the strong V of her
upper back which could almost be a line but the twin dimples
above her buttocks which tremble slightly holding the pose
and the ridges of muscles almost in profile as they twist and
the partial globe of one breast behind latissimus dorsi also.

They fill the air with the air of the place where the chalk light of
the new leaves and poplar bark give way to the paired
floodlights of spring like Robin's bathroom the winter previous
filled with candles as she climbing out of the shower and onto me
in utter warm slipperiness while the artist explains about
"*archetypes*," "*discovered by a psychologist named Carl Jung*" and
his concern for "*the model's 'sense of participation*'" and after much
more *work* by the time he presses her against a wall with a
mattress skeleton for a photograph of a nipple struggling to break
free of wires I can see how liberated her body is from its identity
as sex object just as Spencer Tunick put it and how liberating it is
how very liberating absolutely.

RECTANGULAR BALES EVOKE MUSKOXEN TO FARM LABOURERS ALSO AWARE OF THE SUN

I've always admired the muskox...
— Olga Costopoulos

1. A tractor/wagon combination
escorted by nine labourers. My first bale loading,
bouncing among the floral denizens of Sleepy Hollow
who submit to our tractor-enhanced presence
with a haze of
new September. The noncalluses on my hands,
neophytic, mark the beginner,
and I have the beginner's mind.

But I want to wear one of those
Allis Chalmers baseball hats. I want to
grunt purposefully. I want
a plunging V sunburn, melanoma on my ears.

> I am thinking, and my thought is triangular,
> of the bale wagon. The bales. The sun. The
> golden pyramid of our labour
> rising up; the gatherers run.

> The hayrake, I think,
> whose path we trace,
> adorned these fields in its former day,
> the wheels in a bicycle parade at a county fair—
> decorated with streamers in the spokes
> turning as if to hypnotize, spiral
> spin before my eyes and
> bump. It flies

and mysteriously, here I lie,
looking at the sky.

2. Haymaking time and the hayrake rotated
weeks ago. Followed by the baler later,
gathering wildflowers and fall grasses,
piquant thistles and an unfortunate
grass snake, trapped like dolphin in a canna tuna.

>On the wagon once again
>stacking. Speed being of the essence. Others lift
>and carry bales wagonwards, a constellation
>of workers rotating around this advancing hub, a
>quantum system, the
>atom post-Bohr with the indeterminateness of—

Ouch! (Binder twine can cut.)

>Here on the wagon my strategy is
>bottom layer crosswise
>outside lengthwise inside crosswise.
>Knit one, purl two, knit one, purl two

and the orange lunchpail sun
beaming down like a two-by-four on
our rolling colony.
Snot plentiful on the hay wagon, rust, alphabet
blocks, tossing, stacking, patterning
along the mowéd rows. Wheels rut, bump.
I glance out
across the fields.

The hairy rectangle crouches balefully against the wind.
Like a muskox.
A muskox! Hardly are those words out
when a vast image out of *Mammals of North America*
troubles my sight: somewhere idyllic on a
distant carapace of tundra, bales
of wool stand in a circle, defiant:

The film's narrator expostulates—

"Ken! what are you staring at? Take the friggin' bale!" A
musk-bale and hay-ox struggle onto the wagon.

        I reflect on this along these lines,
        imagining them, winter feed of
        southern cattle, this
        muskox-
        feed of winter cattle, and
        in the warm barn this winter coming, someone
        —me perhaps—forking furry
        horn-crowned bales through feed-chutes,
        clouds of bovine steam arising

        —this my rumination prefiguring
        a future ruminant feeding
        on a figurative ruminant—

But that could never happen in our country.

3. "Suffer the scattered muskoxen
to come to me!" cries a voice
from the bale wagon (my own).
The herd assembles like Toyotas on a transport truck.
Sun exhales in the flailing dust.

> Such the opulence of these surroundings,
> such as crowds out memories
> of the traditional muskox tundra diet,
> as musky foragers gorge
> on alfalfa and clover, the wealth of temperate
> climes, deep green of
> Ontario grasses, stop-action advancement of the
> southern sun. High spray of
> weeds, arched fountains of leaf
> undreamed on the Ellesmere highlands,
> archetypal forests of a primeval landscape
> lost in the muskoxic genetic memory...

Binder twine tentacles grope and entangle
the hemisphere, encompassing the sun,
drawing it
into our community, closer and closer.

Rut in the field. (No not that kind!) Bump.
Tilt, pitch, yaw.
The assembled muskoxen buffalo-jump from the wagon, reassume
feeding formation. The driver turns, swears from the tractor-seat.

Wool-bearing mammals will safely graze.

This was bound to happen. Bound to.

REPLY TO TIM LILBURN'S "QUILL LAKE" BUT ADDRESSED TO TREVOR HERRIOT, WHO WAS THERE THAT DAY TOO (AFTER BEDE AND BEOWULF)

Into this Heorot, Herriot, with its flaming hearth of sun beating against the gleaming tables of sand, into this Heorot it is no mere sparrow who flutters in beneath the eaves, Master, from the long darkness wherein the ice lies heavy on the blackened twigs, where dried berries sparkle, magnified, in their frozen casings, whence briefly we shelter with alkali mead horns overflowing onto our burred beards.

O Herriot,
this is a parliament
you best could denominate—
a toccata of phalarope, killdeer,
widgeon, sandpiper, avocet, curlew, redwing blackbird,
and the proud galleons of pelican ruddering the sky's ogives,
their distant isle peppered with cormorants
like a field of lost puffballs.

No this flock is pouring,
haemorrhaging into the gap under the ridgepole,
the sheer weight of the voices
in waves, palpating hyoids, crescendoing to a
seething immutability of sound beyond Ockeghem or Ligeti,
wheeling above the burnished tables on the
blind updrafts of shimmering beach thermals,
this brief blink of spring before they whirlpool out
in a torrent under the eaves, leaving
their blue silhouette eidetic on our irises,
their great universal polychord
imprinted on our minds.

The birch in dire need of exfoliation, dermabrasion,
curling gold leaf of the bark of illuminated lettering
mouthed in the pure mood of the day.

How the sky decides.
Deicide?

You sit on the lawn.

The winds are all around you.

Fruit bats hang from the trees, their noses arching into updrafts.

There is a golden fish in the sky, scales
raining down to infill the gleaming world:

backdrop to the Byzantine Christ of the birch.

"The Bat House"

The East Coast Swing is a swing dance, the basic pattern of which is Tri-ple-step, tri-ple-step, rock-step.

The spheres described here are based on the layers of earth's atmosphere: there are spheres of glass, light, bugs and bats (Chiroptera).

"Essays on Tick Ontogeny"

Ontic: really existing physically

Ontogeny: the developmental history of an individual organism

Pseudo-Dionysius was a fifth- or sixth-century mystic whose writings were once thought to be from apostolic times.

The Cloud of Unknowing is a fourteenth-century book on contemplative prayer.

"Notes on the Urban Hare"

Hares don't live in burrows, but in rudimentary nests, which are called *forms*. A group of hares was called a *down* in venery.

"Voici le soir charmant, ami du criminel" is the first line of Baudelaire's "Le Crépuscule du soir."

Montana's is a restaurant chain, the logo of which used to feature an illuminated mountainscape.

"The Cherry Tree in Toronto"

Refers to the story of Coyote and the Elk Skull, where coyote bumps into a series of trees (including the cherry) before falling in a creek.

Weeping tile is porous plastic pipe, usually corrugated.

"Notes on the Stomack"

The Aristophanes in this poem is the character in Plato's *Symposium*.

Horrificque is a reference to François Rabelais' *Gargantua*. The full title is *La vie très horrificque du grand Gargantua, père de Pantagruel, jadis composée par M. Alcofribas, abstracteur de quinte essence. Livre plein de pantagruélisme.*

Ding-an-sich (the thing in itself) was written about by Immanuel Kant.

Quid est (what is it) is a Latin phrase associated with Scholastic philosophy.

Waldsea Lake, which once lapped against one of Saskatchewan's loveliest beaches, has since been allowed to flood and no longer exists.

Bedaine is Quebec French and means gut or beer belly.

"The Agon of the Feet"

The Victoria Park in this poem is in Regina.

Saul of Tarsus became the Apostle Paul. There is a tradition that has him riding a horse when Jesus met him and struck him blind. It is not canonical.

The first few lines of Section 5 are misquotations of the *Song of Songs* from the Bible. The section is based on chapter 5 of that book.

Charles Koechlin (1867–1950) was a French composer. *Le Livre de la jungle* is perhaps his best-known work.

"The Aspen"

The China Brain thought experiment is a conceived situation in which each person in China performs the actions of a single neuron. The question is asked whether China could then be described as having consciousness.

"Notes on the Forest"

I took the idea of Aufklärung (*Enlightenment*) from Heidegger.

Serpentinizing is a geological process that turns rocks from earth's mantle into serpentines, some of which are pretty green rocks.

"The Summer of Storms"

Albert Street is a big, fast-moving commercial strip running from Regina's north to south ends.

Taylor Field is now called Mosaic Stadium. The Saskatchewan Roughriders play there.

Davidson and Watrous are southeast of Saskatoon — at one time the highway was left unmaintained for years and years.

"Prolegomenon to the Inhabitation of Trees"

The 120th Avenue in the poem is in Grande Prairie.

"Come Again, Sweet Love Doth Now Invite" is by John Dowland (1563–1626).

"The Sun and I"

The heliosphere is the region of space dominated by the Sun. The Sun is a star of the G2V stellar class.

The twins of a gazelle and so on are from *The Song of Songs*.

Yé-yé is a kind of French popular music that was big in the 1960s.

The reference is to *Poème Symphonique* for 100 mechanical metronomes by the Hungarian composer György Ligeti (1993–2006). It is not particularly typical of his work, although he was one of the first to use controlled randomness in his music.

"Jerry's Barbershop: an Investigation"

The Engelbert Humperdinck in this poem is the Anglo-Indian popular singer.

"Où sont les neiges d'antan" (Where are the snows of yesteryear?) is the refrain from poem "Ballade des dames du temps jadis" by François Villon (1431–1464).

"Extinct Species"

I may be exaggerating how many passenger pigeons there were. One authority claimed they made up between twenty-five and forty per cent of the US bird population.

"Dialogue of Two Maples"

The second last line is kind of stolen from Robert Herrick's "To Lar."

"Reply to Tim Lilburn's 'Quill Lake' but Addressed to Trevor Herriot, Who Was There That Day Too (after Bede and Beowulf)"

Tim Lilburn's poem "Quill Lake" is in his book *Moosewood Sandhills*, which is out of print.

Trevor Herriot is a Saskatchewan writer and naturalist.

The Venerable Bede (c. 672–735) tells the story of the sparrow fluttering into a mead hall in his *The Ecclesiastical History of the English People*.

ACKNOWLEDGEMENTS

The editor of record is Paul Vermeersch. The first version of the manuscript was edited by Erin Mouré and a later one by Don McKay.

Many people helped me with the poems (sometimes obliquely) or persuaded me to cut or include things. Here are a few of their names: Elaine Huth, Louisa Blair, Mariianne Mays, Jan Zwicky, Neal Evans, Dennis Lee, Notes from the Underground Writers Group, Bert Almon, Liz Philips, Alain Richards, Jennifer Eagle, Sherrie Ritchie, Sue Sinclair, Jacky Sawatsky, Ann Stevenson, Lorna Crozier, Maureen Scott-Harris, Anne McDonald (of Regina), Shelley Sopher, Dave Seymour, Steve McOrmond, Matthew Tierney, Charmane Lau, Adrienne Barrett, Ven Begamudré, Katie Martin, Rae Crossman, Gerry Hill, Ken Babstock, Alex Noga, Enrique Hernandez, Brad Martin, Celeste Hernandez, Jane Southwell Munroe, Peg Evans, Paul Wilson, Tim Lilburn, Roo Borson, Kim Maltman, Donna Kane, Wayne Howe, Jody Farrell, Sue Goyette, Anne Simpson and Jean Howe.

The author received support while writing this book from the Saskatchewan Arts Board, the Canada Council and the Ontario Arts Council.

Earlier incarnations of certain poems were published in *Arc, The New Quarterly, Grain, The Malahat Review, Lichen* and other journals too, maybe.

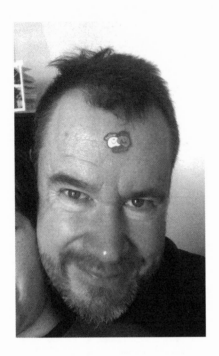

KEN HOWE is a dyed-in-the-wool Québécois born in Edmonton, who moved north to the idyllic town of Beaverlodge at age nine. He studied horn (a.k.a. French horn) performance in university and later became a Jesuit novice. Still later he landed a job as principal horn of the Regina Symphony, where he remained for eight years before being fired just as his first poetry collection, *Household Hints for the End of Time*, was being released. He now lives in Quebec City and has a fun job as a translator. His tenuous hold on sanity is ensured by his wife, E., and their son, Zachary.

DATE DUE